The

HUNGER

of the Heart

The

HUNGER

of the Heart

A Call to Spiritual Growth

✳

Ron DelBene
with Herb & Mary Montgomery

UPPER
ROOM BOOKS
NASHVILLE

THE HUNGER OF THE HEART
Revised Edition

Cover Design by Bruce Gore
Cover Photograph by Westlight/ © Craig Aurness
First Printing: October 1992 (7)
Library of Congress Catalog Number: 92-80945
ISBN: 0-8358-0667-7

Printed in the United States of America

For all of you
who have felt
the hunger of the heart

C O N T E N T S

P R E F A C E

Ron DelBene and I first became acquainted through a publishing house for which we both worked. At the time, he was their national consultant in religious education, and I was an editor. Since then we have followed separate paths. Ron is now an ordained priest in the Episcopal church, and I am an independent writer. He lives in the South and I live in the North. Despite all the changes that have taken place in our lives, we have remained close friends.

Over the years I have followed Ron's personal odyssey as he moved on to new commitments and new challenges. His journey has taken him into campus ministry and participation in renewal movements. After experiencing success in the business world, he became an ordained priest, and for thirteen years has been active in parish ministry. Spiritual direction has long been at the heart of Ron's ministry. In addition to giving spiritual direction privately, he has traveled extensively to give conferences and lead retreats on spiritual development. All Ron's endeavors lend themselves to broadening and deepening his own spirituality. The sum of his experiences gives him a special empathy for those who are struggling to find a more meaningful life of faith.

Ron encourages those seeking spiritual direction to record their thoughts in journals, which they then share with him. In the deeply felt reflections of the journals he found similar themes that suggested there might be specific and identifiable stages of spiritual growth that people pass through. Conferences and seminars he conducted provided the perfect opportunity to present his ideas about the stages of spiritual development. Once he began to share his insights, it became obvious that he had found a way to describe the quest for spirituality in a form that was comprehensible to both those with a little religious experience and those with a lot. As he began giving the stages descriptive names, members of his audience nodded knowingly and were eager to share their own stories. These experiences confirmed what Ron already believed to be true, and out of this background was born *The Hunger of the Heart*.

The journal entries found throughout the book help illustrate the stages. All the entries are used with the permission of the authors, and their contribution is gratefully acknowledged. The entries appear as they were written. However, names and certain identifying details have been changed to protect the privacy of the individuals.

The Hunger of the Heart, The Breath of Life: A Simple Way to Pray, and *Alone with God: A Guide for Personal Retreats* have all been previously published. All three were books I encouraged Ron to write and on which I served as his mentor, critic, and editor. The books enjoyed a long life, but eventually needed to be updated. Because they were still very much in demand, Upper Room Books chose to reissue them. My wife, Mary, who is also a writer, joined Ron and me in updating and revising these books that have proven their worth by standing the test of time. The three of us thank Janice Lilly for reading the series and making editorial suggestions.

Preface

Wherever you are in your spiritual life, *The Hunger of the Heart* will give you a better understanding of your yearning to draw closer to God. In these pages you will find the encouragement needed to either embark on your spiritual journey, or to remain steadfast on the journey you have already begun.

HERB MONTGOMERY

Called to Wholeness

"I invite you to begin thinking of yourself as a pilgrim."

✳

Why do I always feel there should be something more to life than I am experiencing?

What can I do to make my relationship with God more satisfying?

How can I get my life together?

These are a few of the questions typically faced by people who come to me seeking spiritual direction. They are questions I have faced myself, and you probably have as well.

Before we examine the stages of spiritual growth that point to some answers, let's recall what God has in mind for us. Scripture tells us that we are called to be whole people who grow into a deeper balance and union with the parts of ourselves, with other people, and with God. Specifically we are told, "You must therefore be perfect just as your heavenly Father is perfect" (Matt. 5:48, JB).

To be perfect as God is perfect? What an unattainable, even unfair expectation—an expectation that puts us in what is commonly referred to as a double bind. Such a bind produces an inner dialogue that goes like this:

I need to be perfect like God.

But you can't be perfect like God.

I have to be! It's right there in Scripture.

But you know you can't.

Even though I know I can't, I must keep trying.

We can alleviate this dilemma by understanding what is meant by the word *perfect*. In the original Greek, it means "whole" or "integrated" or "together." For most people, this opens an entirely new way of looking at their spiritual potential.

Consider your own life. Surely there have been times when you have felt that everything was going well, when you were a whole person with your life moving in the proper direction. You were together, integrated in mind, body, and spirit. You were functioning as one, functioning as God intends.

For some people the potential for a rich spiritual life is damaged because perfection, as they understand it, is unattainable. Jean was such a person. When she came to see me, she was a wife and mother in her early thirties and confronting the issue of always having to be perfect. Worry about being perfect had begun in early childhood. In her journal, Jean wrote about her troubling history:

> I was afraid because I knew what would happen when I brought home a report card with five A's and one B. And it did. The first comment from my father was "Why the B?" So the next grading period I really wanted to "prove" myself. I worked very hard and came home with six A's.
>
> I was so proud. I knew I had made it. But what was the first response of my father? "Must have been an easy term. Don't let it go to your head. Your class is probably not too smart."

So there I was! I couldn't win. I remember that time so very well. Maybe that's when I decided that I was a loser. And that was only one instance of many times when I felt I had to live up to something that I couldn't. And I remember crying about that.

Then I remember the church just adding to that with more about how I needed to be perfect. Wow, I spent my whole life trying to be perfect for my father and never making it, and now God was asking me to be perfect. I was a loser even before I really started.

When I heard that perfect really means whole or integrated, I got a new lease on life. . . . Suddenly it was like God was a part of my life. My own integration was what God was talking about. At that moment I was just filled with God's love. What freedom! The truth really does make you free.

Whereas some people have their spiritual development warped by the mistaken understanding of perfection, others fall victim to the "ladder mentality." Early in the Christian tradition of spirituality, the ladder became a popular image symbolizing our growth toward God. Such an image was consistent with the prevailing understanding of God as being "up there" (in heaven) and we were "down here" (on earth). Our responsibility was to get up there to God.

In times past, the ladder image was effective because it was both easy to visualize and to understand. Today we realize that this image did not fully take into account that God had already "come down" and become one of us in the person of Jesus. No longer was there a need to get "up there" to God.

The ladder image also suggested that spiritual growth means rising, step-by-step, to an ever higher level. (The song "We Are Climbing Jacob's Ladder"— "higher, higher"—is based on the image of the ladder in Genesis 28:12.) We have inherited the idea that the higher we go, the better we are. Certainly it is true that through such activities as prayer, Christian meditation, ministry to others, and study of the Scriptures we grow spiritually. But if we hold to the ladder image, we are in danger of being unduly concerned with where we are in relation to others. Are we ahead of someone else? Are others ahead of us? Often we hear judgments, and perhaps even make them ourselves, about who is where on the ladder leading heavenward.

In place of the ladder image, I offer the tree as a more appropriate symbol for our time. At any given moment a tree is complete. If you plant a tree that is two inches in diameter, you don't say, "I planted half a tree today." A tree is a tree no matter what the size. The difference between a tree that is two inches in diameter and one that is twenty inches is that one has been around longer than the other.

So it is with us. God did not create just half a you or half a me. From the moment of our birth, each of us is complete. At times our growth is more rapid than at other times, but at every point in our lives we are whole.

The tree, too, has periods when growth is more evident. This is apparent when the tree is cut down and the growth rings inside the trunk are visible. Some rings are wide, indicating a time when growth was intense. Other rings are narrow, indicating that growth was slight. These growth rings can be likened to the stages in our spiritual lives. There are growing times when we seem especially close to God. Then there are those times when we feel stunted spiritually; we sense very little growth and wonder if we are standing still or maybe even back-sliding. Yet even in those seemingly arid times, growth is still occurring.

Martin, whom I first met in his early twenties, was impatient with his spiritual growth and never satisfied with his progress. The tree image was especially helpful for him in realizing how a person can be both whole and growing. In one of Martin's journal entries he wrote:

> When I heard that I am complete now, I immediately thought, no I'm not. Then the more I thought about it, the more I see what you mean. I was never pleased with my prayer life, with my walk with God, the spiritual good I was doing. I always had to be better. Now I see that I am where I am supposed to be. That's a relief. I can begin to enjoy where I am. I know I'm alive and growing, but I'm no longer running.

The call to wholeness is also a call to holiness. For Christians, the two are inseparable. Scripture calls us to:

- death and new life (Rom. 6:4)
- sin no more (John 5:14)
- pray unceasingly (Eph. 6:18)
- make peace (Matt. 5:9)
- feed the hungry and clothe the naked (Matt. 25:31-46).

Despite the incidents of violence and human alienation reported daily in the media, I believe that more people than ever are hearing the call to perfection, the call to wholeness. Look around your own neighborhood or community and you will find people responding to God's call to love and to be of service. They are joining in prayer groups, working in soup kitchens, participating in fund drives, and ministering to broken hearts and battered spirits.

What about you? Do you have a desire to draw closer to God and to those whose lives you touch? Perhaps as you celebrate yet another birthday, you feel an inner nudge to focus more on your spiritual life. Or the invitation might become apparent as you work with a therapist, counselor, or spiritual director who helps you discover an untapped dimension of yourself. The call could be as gentle as a whisper while reading the Scriptures or as noisy as a shout of outrage when you see an abused child.

As Christians we are called to be whole, called to lead lives of care and concern. So I invite you to begin thinking of yourself as a pilgrim—a person who freely chooses to join in the continuing journey of spiritual growth. In the chapters that follow, we will travel that road together.

> Happy are the people whose strength is in you!
> Whose hearts are set on the pilgrim's way.
> Psalm 84:4
> *Book of Common Prayer*, 1979

CHAPTER 2

The Awakening Stage
"There must be something more. . . ."

✳

Have you ever been up late watching TV and felt drawn to the refrigerator? You open the door and stare absently inside while the cold rushes at your feet. You don't know what will be satisfying, but finally pick out something to eat. In a few minutes you are back in the kitchen to get something to drink, thinking that was what you wanted all along. At last you are full—too full—and realize you weren't really hungry or thirsty after all.

The first stage in the journey of spiritual growth is something like that. But instead of the hunger being physical, it is a hunger of the heart. Many people ignore this crucial moment of awakening because they don't understand what is happening to them. It is a stage that can be both distressing and depressing because no matter what we do, our life just isn't what we once thought it was meant to be. Confusion. Unrest. Dissatisfaction. These are but three of the most common feelings at this time.

John, a family man with a comfortable home and a good job in sales, reflected this stage. Although he had a number of reasons to feel fulfilled, he was unhappy with everything about his life. His work no longer challenged him. He was eating and drinking too much and found himself lighting one cigarette with another. At home, such trivial matters as the slam of a door or a bike left in the driveway caused him to blow up. In John's daydreams he imagined himself escaping to California where he could begin a new life—and this time get it right.

Although John didn't know it yet, he was longing for something much more satisfying than the comfortable lifestyle he had worked so hard to attain. He was yearning for a deeper relationship with God; yearning for the spiritual dimension that would give meaning not just to his work or home life but to his *entire* life.

As I got to know John better, I found that he really did love his wife and children and enjoyed his job. Looking at the individual parts of his life, he couldn't see anything seriously wrong. Yet in his heart John recognized that something critical was missing. What he had been ignoring was the call to bring all the aspects of his life into focus around God.

For a moment let's consider what we mean by God. We know that God is our Creator (Genesis 1); God is love (1 John 4:8); God is the one who loves us enough to send Jesus to save us from our sins (John 3:16). Unfortunately, these images are difficult to picture. For those who find God abstract and God's presence difficult to imagine, I suggest thinking of God as did Abba Dorotheus, a spiritual director at the beginning of the seventh century. This is what he said to his students:

> Imagine a circle with its centre and radii or rays going out from this centre. The further these radii are from the centre the more widely are they dispersed and separated from one an-

other. . . . Suppose now that this circle is the world, the very centre of the circle, God, and the lines (radii) going from the centre to the circumference or from the circumference to the centre are the paths of [people's] lives.*

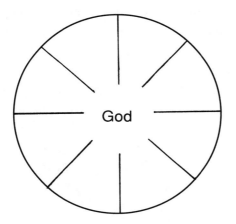

The diagram helps us visualize how we can move either away from or toward God. The choice is ours to make. It also suggests that the nearer we come to God, the closer we come to one another.

Even though we might ignore the hunger of the heart or misinterpret its meaning, it keeps returning. For many people, the first awareness of the hunger is no more than a restlessness, or sense of dis-ease. Tom's awakening occurred one ordinary morning as he looked in the mirror

---

* *Early Fathers from the Philokalia,* translated by E. Kadloubovsky and G. E. H. Palmer (London: Faber & Faber, 1954), pages 164-165.

while shaving and blurted, "There must be something more to life than this!"

For Betty, an accountant, the awakening came in the middle of lunch one day when a friend casually asked, "How do you feel about God?" Later Betty told me that at that moment she felt as though a burden had been lifted from her. Something as simple as a friend's question made her realize that she had to take responsibility for her spiritual life.

In an attempt to offset the hunger of the heart, some people plunge into work or recreation or drugs with such determination that what begins as dis-ease ends up being disease. Workaholism is an example of what happens when someone refuses to acknowledge the importance of developing as a whole person. Marriages deteriorate, children grow up without really knowing their workaholic parent, and interests that would enrich the workaholic's life go unexplored.

Often the hunger of the heart is experienced as the desire to get something more *out* of life. While there's nothing wrong with that, the hunger of the heart is really a reminder to bring something more *into* life. That something more is an ongoing relationship with God and an ever-deepening faith.

What I have said thus far may seem to apply only to non-Christians, or to Christians whose relationship with God has lapsed. This is not the case. Even a totally committed Christian can experience a sense of dis-ease, a feeling of being dissatisfied and unfulfilled. Why? Because *this stage, as well as the other stages on the pilgrim's way, may be passed through time and time again.*

Remember that spiritual growth is not like a ladder that we climb to be "up there" with God. Rather, our growth is better symbolized by the tree that is complete at all times. As the tree grows in every direction, its roots must go deeper in order to provide stability and supply the necessary nutrients. So it is with us. We, too, must be growing in many different ways, and the hunger of the heart is our call to grow. It is a sign that God is calling us to send our roots deeper and deeper.

A number of years ago I was working for a Christian publishing house and living in a way that I believed was right for my family and for me. I was in a helping profession and was confident that I was doing my job well. In spite of that, I sensed the need to be doing something more. As a result, I chose to become more attentive to my prayer life, and for a time that was very satisfying. Yet once again I felt the hunger of the heart. Then a struggle began within me. Did God really want me to move to a more simple lifestyle and commit myself to working in the area of spiritual growth? I tried for a time to avoid the question and be satisfied where I was. But God had other plans for me, and no matter what I did, I remained dissatisfied. After a long period of reflection, I surrendered to the fact that this was a time of awakening for me, and I said yes to God. Our family moved and I began work at the Hermitage, a place where people could come to study, reflect, and pray under my guidance. Although you might think that would be the end to my heart's hunger, it was really only the beginning.

In the more than twenty years since then there have been times when my heart has been hungry, and I have moved again through the awakening and other stages to discover more about the next chapter in my life and ministry. These experiences have taught me that the hunger of the heart is never an ending. Rather, it is always a beginning. Either it is an opportunity to let God into our lives for the first time, or it is a chance to move further along the path of spiritual growth with God at our side.

Properly understood, the hunger of the heart is an awakening. It is the stage at which we realize God is calling us to wholeness and fullness of life (Eph. 1:3-7). When Sharon, an office worker in an auto dealership, came to me, her life had been narrowly focused on a disappointing love relationship—a relationship she thought was the one thing meant to make her happy. Soon she realized that romantic love was not what she truly needed at this point in her life. In her journal she made this entry:

> I don't know where all this is leading me, but I know my "heart-burn" continues to increase. I thought a new job would take care of it, but my heart isn't in it. I am functioning. I am doing what needs to be done, but it is a struggle, because I am not committed. I need to be committed, to believe. . . .

Sharon's moment of awakening was not the first time God had been active in her life. It was, however, the first time she had been aware of it and realized that now she had to make her response.

Have you ever experienced—or are you now experiencing—the hunger of the heart? If so, recognize it as

God's call to move into a journey in spiritual growth that will involve many stages.

C H A P T E R 3

The Seeking Stage
"I longed to know God."

✳

Jack's parents divorced when he was a child and that left him with many unresolved feelings. Even as a young adult, Jack found it difficult to believe in the permanence of anything. Though recently graduated and newly employed, he realized his heart hungered for something, and a moment of awakening led him to become an active seeker.

When Jack and I first met, he still wore the look of elation so commonly associated with this stage of growth. Seekers are excited about the potential the future holds for them. They see possibilities instead of problems and are eager to get on with the journey. Often they move rapidly from one activity to another, trying to find *the* answer. This is how Jack described what was happening to him during the seeking stage:

> I began the round of self-improvements: self-awareness with groups, alone, reading . . . with a deep need for spiritual development. I longed to know God, as I felt that true unconditional love of the Master would free me from turmoil. I longed for the mystical experience.

If we compare Jack's journal entry with the words of the psalmist, we find that seeking closeness with God unites us with our faith ancestors:

As a deer longs for flowing streams,
so my soul longs for you, O God.
My soul thirsts for God,
for the living God.
When shall I come and behold
the face of God?
Psalm 42:1-2

During the seeking stage, the words *yearning,* or *longing* are often used. It is a stage in which there is a sense of wanting something to happen, and wanting it to happen *now.* This yearning may also be accompanied by apprehension; we fear that what we want so much will fail to appear.

When people come to me seeking help in finding God's will for themselves, I share with them that the word *will,* which we translate from the Latin *voluntas,* means "yearning" in both Hebrew and Greek. To ask "What is God's will for me?" is the same as asking "What is God's yearning for me?" To satisfy the hunger of the heart is to satisfy the deep yearning God has awakened within us.

While an undefined yearning characterizes the awakening stage, in the seeking stage, the yearning begins to clarify itself and there is hope that it will be satisfied. Seekers often report feelings of being led, and an inability (or unwillingness) to turn back. However we describe the experience, I believe it is the Spirit of God calling us closer, loving us as no one else ever can or will. Such love is beyond our human experience, which may be why we are so slow to recognize it.

If we agree that God is like the parent of the prodigal child, yearning for our return to the fullness in and for which we were created, then we begin to see that we are not alone. Nor are we on a journey never traveled before. You and I are but two of the many travelers who have heard the ancient call, sensed the yearning, and set forth. Although the journey is new to us, it is one that all holy people have made. In one of the apostle Paul's letters to the early believers, we glimpse how the Spirit of God draws us to greater wholeness:

> These things God has revealed to us through the Spirit; for the Spirit searches everything, even the depths of God. For what human being knows what is truly human except the human spirit that is within? So also no one comprehends what is truly God's except the Spirit of God. Now we have received not the spirit of the world, but the Spirit that is from God, so that we may understand the gifts bestowed on us by God.
>
> 1 Corinthians 2:10-12

Seeking is the result of having been awakened to experience God's Spirit. It is both a stage shared by all seekers and a stage in which each of us seeks according to our individual need. Although the inner journey may seem easy at first, seekers soon discover that along with the freedom to make our own decisions, we also have the freedom to make our own mistakes.

Knowing what is involved in each stage of spiritual growth is helpful, but it does not insure that the journey will always be smooth. Detours, bumps, and occasional roadblocks are to be expected. What do we do when these occur? How do we keep on the path we have chosen for ourselves? The answer lies in self-discipline. Some people find the need for discipline unsettling and even threatening. Those who are fearful of assuming personal responsibility for their spiritual growth tend to search for a dogmatic leader or the kind of church that will do their thinking for them. In this area, I advise caution.

Persons at the seeking stage are very vulnerable. Often this vulnerability is manifested in a wonderful openness toward others. New pilgrims have a tendency to project their honesty onto those they meet and may naively put their trust in teachers or groups that are subtly seductive. Cults are adept at recognizing seekers and drawing them into physical and mental submission. Though the young are especially vulnerable, more experienced pilgrims may be victimized as well. During the seeking stage, idealism can be so heightened that the seeker accepts a religious doctrine without question. To examine a new belief system, a seeker can ask these questions:

- Is this way found in Scripture?
- Is this a way that seeks to be inclusive and not exclusive?
- Has it been present throughout the history of the Christian church?
- Do followers have a commitment to social justice?
- Does the belief system make a person more loving?

• Does it help a person focus on the human needs of others?

If the answer is yes to all these questions, then the way is probably of God and will lead you on the right path.

While advising caution in the seeking stage, I also want to point out that joyful surprises are in store. The seeker may join a prayer group and find unexpected friendship. Sharing and discussing our spiritual journey with other pilgrims is a particular delight. The support and enthusiasm of others fuels the desire to continue.

During this time, the Spirit is leading the seeker to prayer and discipline. To those who ask, "How do I start a disciplined prayer life?" I recommend the breath prayer. It is not a prayer that uses other people's words but rather is a short, personal prayer that we each discover for ourselves. This prayer that can be said as easily and naturally as breathing lies like a tiny seed within us, and when nurtured, grows and flowers into a new closeness to with God. To learn how to discover your breath prayer see "The Breath Prayer" on page 107 of this book.

CHAPTER 4

The Learning Stage

"When the disciple is ready, the teacher appears."

✳

To move beyond the seeking stage, we must have a teacher. At this point, however, the teacher is not necessarily a person. The teacher may be a book, a movie, a line from scripture, a dream, a waking vision, or something else that we recognize as having special significance for our spiritual growth.

One day I was reading the gospel for the following Sunday and considering how I would present the core of the message in my next sermon. My usual practice is to read the gospel lessons each day and reflect on them. Then as I go through the week, the meaning shifts and new ideas appear. This particular week was not a good one for me. Each day as I tried to focus on the gospel, my attention slipped back to myself and a disagreement I had with Julie, a parishioner. On Friday as I read the story in the quiet of my study, I grumbled aloud, "Who put *that* line in there?" Even though I had read that same scripture four times, I had not seen the words "their minds were closed." On the fifth reading, they stood out boldly.

That day I was the disciple ready to hear. I understood the message and realized that my mind had been closed. If I wanted to begin to resolve the situation I had been ignoring, I could open my mind by asking Julia to share her thoughts with me.

While in that instance scripture was my teacher, Sandra was at a point in her journey where her teacher needed to be a person. Although Sandra was an intelligent and attractive young woman, she didn't perceive these qualities in herself. She had few friends and no one with whom to share her innermost concerns. This is how she expressed the situation in her journal:

> What does it matter to me? It matters that there isn't anyone in my life who cares about butterflies. You see, there was this butterfly up on the mountain with me. It had brown velvet wings with orange silk trim and it did a splendid ballet among the rocks and trees. Then it landed on my shoe and sat still for a long time. But there was no one to share my butterfly.
>
> Then Jane, a friend who sensed the depth of my seeking and yearning, suggested I call Ron. I didn't even know him, or what he did. It seemed that I had tried everything else and was ready to grasp at any straw that was offered.

Soon after writing that passage, Sandra acted on her need to meet someone who would understand her yearning. "At that point I was ready," Sandra told me, "but as I look back now, I guess I wouldn't have been ready before that."

A parallel can be drawn between our spiritual journey and that of the Israelites who wandered for forty years in the desert. Their yearning and their seeking were, as we read in scripture, a purification:

For the Israelites travelled in the wilderness for forty years, until the whole nation, all the fighting men among them, had passed away, all who came out of Egypt and had disobeyed the voice of the Lord.

Joshua 5:6, NEB

So it is in our journey. All the fighting within to get somewhere by our own design, all the disobedience of knowing the inner voice of God yet choosing to do something else must pass away. Only when the new creation is within us will we truly enter into meeting the teacher as did Mark, a middle-aged counselor who came to see me. A disciplined runner who was very concerned about his physical fitness, Mark was just beginning to see that he had spiritual needs and wasn't sure how to meet them. This led to frustrations that caused problems at home. He became impatient with his family and made unreasonable demands on his children. Mark described the struggle in this journal entry:

I had been seeking someone for a long time, but not really. I knew that it was inevitable, but it seems now when I look back on it that there were parts of me that had to be "cleaned out" before it could come about. I guess for the past year and a half, I have been recognizing parts of myself which I needed to let go of if I really wanted to grow.

When the disciple is ready, the teacher does indeed appear. The teacher, however, may not say anything new. Often the message is one we have heard before, sometimes not just once, but many times. The difference is that now we are spiritually ready—we have, as scripture states, the ears to hear and the eyes to see (Matt. 13:13-17). In reporting his reaction to my direction, Mark wrote:

> Surprisingly enough, you said nothing that I hadn't heard many times, but I suddenly heard it in stereo at high volume. I was surrounded by the words. It was holy ground, and it was really as if God was speaking. I guess you could say you were a burning bush to me.

Another example of spiritual readiness occurred when I was teaching a class on unceasing prayer. One of the students was a silver-haired gentleman who kept nodding his agreement as I spoke. Afterward he introduced himself and said, "Tonight was like Pentecost Sunday to me. I heard you talking my language. You don't know how long I've waited to hear someone else speak what I've been saying to myself for years. Thank you."

Some pilgrims quickly reach the stage at which the teacher appears. Others, like the elderly gentleman in my class, wander in the desert for years. No matter how short or how extended the period of time, it invariably seems too long.

Timothy was a young priest whose wanderings, though intense, lasted only a short time. In his journal he recounted an experience that helped him understand this stage of his journey:

I was sitting quietly, and the story of Lazarus came to mind, especially the moment when Jesus weeps, sighs, and calls Lazarus forth. Then I felt myself enclosed in a tomb and I found myself removing layers, like blankets. At the first layer, I asked for forgiveness for the self-idolatry. . . . Then came a deeper cover. I was reluctant to touch it, but I did. I pulled it off and a deep sigh came from my heart. Suddenly I was at a door—the same door that I had tried to open before. This time I gave it a hearty yank and it opened easily. Light fell in upon me immediately. An arm beckoned me to go through the door into this unknown world. I did, and I felt an embrace throughout my body. Then there was silence.

I see now a new revelation from the story of Lazarus. We are all Lazarus bound up by the wraps of our own death and sin. In the aloneness of our hearts we hear the voice cry, "Come out!" We peel the wrappings that bind us and stumble for the door and into the daylight of life and the loving arms of Jesus.

Timothy's new awareness prepared him to continue his journey. His recollection of the experience helps us see that when we are ready, the teacher appears. Whether the teacher be a person, a book, a movie, a line from Scripture, a dream, a waking vision, or another event that reshapes our thinking is unimportant. What matters is that we are ready. Then when we hear God call our name, we, like Samuel, have the opportunity to answer, "Here I am" (1 Sam. 3:1-10).

CHAPTER 5

The Relief, Anger, Fear Stage
"But my God, I am so fearful."

✳

At those times when the spiritual journey seems all uphill, the recognition that a teacher can help us brings relief. This sense of relief is a sign that we are moving along and have reached a new stage—that of relief, anger, and fear. The relief we felt at finding a teacher turns out to be transitory, and as Emily's story illustrates, we often experience anger and fear.

At twenty-six, Emily had a history of being rejected. Even though she had been hurt, she refused to be bitter, choosing instead to continue a search for a community where she would find acceptance. Her most recent rejection had occurred when she told some members of her church about a vision she had experienced. A man in the group immediately suggested that she needed counseling. Although Emily probably could have benefited from such help, she had expected understanding from the group, not advice. She believed that other Christians would understand and appreciate her feelings, and when they didn't, she once again felt the sting of rejection.

I happened to meet Emily on the rebound. Fortunately, she was still open to God's love and eager to make sense of her confusing experiences. Keeping a journal helped her gain a new perspective, as we see in this excerpt from her early writings:

> I have been going around for the past few years, just searching out someone or someplace where I could know that I belonged. This morning at church, I came home. It has been a long journey, but now I am home. What a relief. I can quit looking.

The great relief Emily felt was short-lived. A few weeks later, an anxious and upset Emily came to my church office and asked if she could see me for a few minutes. I invited her in and had no more than closed the door when she shouted, "Where were you when I needed you? Why did it take me so long to find this place? Why can't the church have more people who care?"

Emily's words rolled like ocean waves in a storm. I had never before met anyone quite this angry about spending so much time seeking and not finding. At last she slumped into a chair. After a deep sigh, she said quietly, "I'm sorry. I don't know why I'm so angry at you. It just all seems so cruel."

I assured Emily that although she might feel that her reaction was confused and inappropriate, it was not unusual. The relief felt at finding a teacher often gives way to anger as seekers reflect on having had to wait so long.

Then I mentioned to Emily that she was also likely to experience fear, the third emotion that can be expected at this stage of spiritual growth. Emily drew back and laughed nervously. "You must have read my mind," she said. "Just last night I was talking with a friend about how exciting it was to find this new support for my walk with God, and I found myself feeling afraid. I couldn't understand it. It was like I wouldn't be in control."

A review of the relief, anger, fear stage shows how logically one emotion follows the other:

- We yearn for something with our whole being.
- We find it and are relieved to know that at last we are not alone.
- We become angry that it took so long to reach that point.
- We experience fear—fear that now we may have to do something.

When people are at the relief, anger, fear stage of their journey, I often share an excerpt from Bob's journal. Though young in years, Bob was old in experiences. He had been heavily into drugs and dropped in and out of one subculture after another. He thought that spending time at the Hermitage was just going to be another experience to add to his repertoire. God, however, had other designs as we see in this entry:

> There is a gentling process taking place. I am very much at peace and feel good about myself. After not feeling good about myself for so long, this is a nice change. I am not trying so hard to have an exceptional experience or hear the voice of God or see an exceptional vision. I am just trying to be. I am only trying to have patient expectations and to let this time heal me. But my God, I am so fearful that something really will happen!

What will I have to do now that I have found someone and someplace that challenges me and takes me seriously? I think that maybe I was better off running around wildly to keep my mind off the call from God that I kept hearing. But I don't remember ever feeling this afraid, even during some of the bad trips on drugs. Fear. Now maybe I'll have to do something. Maybe that's why the apostles were so often fearful.

When Emily finished reading this journal excerpt, she put it down and said, "I know what he means."

Many people stay in a given stage for months or even years. For them, spiritual growth is rather like business that is begun but never really tended to. This was true of Dolores, a priest in her early forties who kept so busy with the problems of her congregation that it was easy to avoid her own needs. She thought that coming to the peacefulness of the Hermitage was simply going to be a rest—a time away from the pressures of her work. The afternoon Dolores arrived, she said it was almost like coming to the ivy-covered cottage of her childhood imaginings. Here was a place to be alone with her dreams, her prayers, and her Bible.

But the next morning Dolores was far from peaceful. When she met me at the door, her face was tense and stern. We sat down opposite one another in the prayer room and Dolores looked at me with blazing eyes. "The whole institutional church stinks!" she cried. "Why did I have to come this far and wait this long to find a place to be alone and pray?"

Dolores's anger was a familiar and understandable part of this stage. In middle age, she was frustrated by the realization that she had been putting off her personal spiritual growth. At first she tried to find someone to blame, which is a usual response. We like to believe that our failure to grow is the fault of our parents, teachers, the pressure of work, or the denomination in which we grew up, all of which do affect us. However, instead of trying to place blame, how much wiser to assess how we were molded, where we are now, and how we are going to proceed on our journey of the spirit.

As time went on in her retreat, a calmer Dolores began to look ahead and see new possibilities. In her journal, she wrote:

> Am I ready to hear God? Ready to do whatever God asks me? Rather frightening! I know myself so well. Will it be something I don't want to give up? I'm afraid. . . .

The way I experience the relief, anger, fear stage is best described in a family story that happened when our children were young. Near our home was a water flume, a huge playground slide built into a hillside. Water gushed down the slide and flume riders zoomed round and round the curves on plastic mats before splash landing in a pool at the bottom. Secretly I wanted very much to ride the flume. When I shared this desire with my children, they soon convinced me it was a great idea, so we set a time for a family outing.

Standing at the top of the flume I had two realizations: the flume was much higher than I thought it would be, and I was facing the unexpected. *Going down? Not me!* But there I stood, unwilling to retreat and scared to go forward. I got angry at myself for wanting to do such a foolish thing. It was an irrational moment. I knew that thousands had made this trip safely and I would too, but....

The line kept getting shorter and shorter. Then it was my turn. Tense as a stretched rubber band, I put the mat down and the flowing water whisked me away. My little mat went so fast that I felt totally out of control. With my hands frozen in a grip, I pulled the front of the mat up, not realizing that doing so gave me even less control. In total panic I spun completely around, forgetting even that there was water at the bottom. Suddenly I made a splash landing and laughed. How easy it was!

So often our life with God is that way. We want to climb to the heights, have the vision, and enjoy the ride, so to speak. But how hard it is to give up control to God and let be what will be.

Not everyone experiences the relief, anger, fear stage in the same way. Depending upon our personality and background, the intensity of each emotion varies. But in this crucial stage of growth we are confronted with the reality as old as the Exodus. Like the Israelites we are relieved to be saved from bondage, then angry that it took so long, and eventually fearful about what the future may hold.

The Doubting Stage

"Doubts are of different kinds and usually come in bunches."

✳

What happens when doubts arise on your spiritual journey? Although this can happen at any stage, it is most likely to occur after encountering a teacher and being challenged by God through that teacher to enter into the journey more actively. At this point we may feel reluctant to go further. There is a temptation to dig in our heels and stay put, or even return to the familiarity of a previous stage.

The doubting stage follows the relief, anger, fear stage, and is a natural outgrowth of fear. While participating in the process of growth and movement into God's loving power, we eventually wonder whether we are doing the right thing. It is new territory with unfamiliar landmarks, and we are understandably wary.

This stage can be likened to an experience our family had years ago on a visit to New York City. From the 102nd floor of the Empire State Building to the second basement of the subway, it is a city of sharp contrasts and immense size. The number of people seated on the main floor of one Broadway theater we attended was greater than the entire population of our hometown!

I remember especially our family's first excursion on the subway. We knew where we wanted to go and had seen on the map of the system which trains to take. Still, there was a bit of hesitation about "really doing it." Finally we made our decision and began the trip. Every time the train stopped, I nervously checked to make sure we were still on the right line. We completed that first trip successfully, and two others as well. After that third trip, I felt secure about where we were going and even gave directions to other tourists.

Parallels can be drawn between that experience and our journey into a deeper relationship with God. As we begin the journey, the territory is strange, and we wonder if we are going in the right direction. Awed by the experience, we proceed with trepidation. What's happening may even overwhelm us. This is natural when moving from the familiar to the unfamiliar.

Just as the subway map helped me find my way in the city, this book is intended to help you find your way through the stages of growth. Soon you will be familiar with the signposts and recognize where you have been, where you are, and where you are going. When that happens, a glow of understanding will give you the confidence to point the way for others who are just beginning the journey.

On every journey doubts arise. They are of different kinds and usually come in bunches:
- Am I on the right track?
- Does anyone else take God seriously?
- Whom should I trust?
- Isn't God too awesome for me to comprehend?
- Is there truly a journey?

- Haven't I just been standing still?
- Why me?

If we let them, doubts will clutter the path and prevent us from moving ahead. It then becomes easy to fall back to an earlier stage that we understand and accept, or as Ellen did, get bogged down right where we are.

At age thirty-four, Ellen was the wife of a successful executive and the mother of three children. Aside from being a busy homemaker, she played an active role in her community. Amid the busyness of her life, Ellen heard her name called much the way Samuel had (1 Sam. 3:1-10). She decided to take some time for reflection and came to the Hermitage where she entered these thoughts in her journal:

> This morning I got up and wondered to myself, what am I doing here? I am panicked in a sense. I began to think of all the people who would think that spending time in solitude in a little place in the middle of a wooded area was crazy. Yet I feel that this is where God is calling me at this point.

A few days later, Ellen had seen through the doubts and recognized them for what they were—defenses against moving ahead in her journey. She went on to write:

> Now I see more clearly why I had not come to the Hermitage before this time. I was not ready. Moreover, I don't think I would have been able to move through the tremendous doubts that I had the other night. I think I would

have gotten out of here and gone home. I see now that the doubts about what I was doing here and the fear that I would probably be thought crazy were all my defenses. Probably for the same reason I brought all my needlework and books and art supplies. I remember thinking I had to bring enough to do in case I got restless. I see now that the restlessness was fear and a defense against hearing the voice of God in the silence of being alone. . . .

Sometimes we are simply not ready to move further along the path of spiritual growth. At other times, we are certain the time is right, and still decide not to go. Excuses that get expressed as doubts are endless. Perhaps the most destructive doubt is one expressed by a young student who said, "I just can't imagine that God would choose me and want me as a friend. I mean, why would God care about me? Who am I?"

Why is it so hard to accept that God loves us unconditionally? Why do so many of us feel we have to earn God's love? Answers may be found at least in part in the way we grew up. As children it is common to feel that we have to earn our parents' love and to please friends and neighbors in order to win their approval. The message we got in childhood is reinforced by a culture that tells us we must perform to be rewarded. Thus we do the things we know will get us the affirmation we desire. We may dress for the approval of others. We may follow a career path to satisfy a parent. We may marry or befriend a person we know we can please. Not surprisingly, when we come to the life with God, we look for ways to earn God's love. And how damaging it is to that spiritual relationship when we begin to doubt that God really loves us.

But God does love us, loves us freely, with no strings. God's love is a gift. All we need do is accept it!

When doubts arise, it is helpful to talk with someone. This is one of the roles spiritual directors have always filled. If no such guide is available to you, try meeting with someone who has previously made the journey. Another helpful thing to do at this stage is to search out reading material that gives you insight into the struggles of others who have sought to know the fullness of God's love. Above all, remember that doubting is a stage we all go through, and that it too shall pass if we are dedicated to the journey we have begun.

CHAPTER 7

The Testing Stage

"I really had to check it out. . . ."

✷

Two clergymen who attended my presentation of prayer at a workshop in the Midwest approached me immediately afterward. I knew from their whispers and skeptical glances that something had unsettled them. Finally one of them said in a halting fashion, "That was . . . ah . . . very interesting, and we were wondering where you took your theological training."

The name tags these clergymen wore indicated they were from a section of the country where it was commonly believed that a certain seminary dean practically "sat at the right hand of God." Smiling to myself I offhandedly said, "Oh, at Marquette University, the same place where Dean _____ got his degree."

My answer brightened the men's faces and they began speaking excitedly about my presentation. Having passed their test for authenticity, they were now eager to speak in more detail about their own spirituality.

Testing or verifying the authenticity of someone we look to for guidance is a necessary step in the process of spiritual growth. When we find someone with whom we "click" or who "speaks our language," we want to be sure they are qualified. Although it is important to be cautious, it is also important that we not measure a person solely on the basis of degree or position. To test for authenticity, I suggest using this question:

• Does the person's lifestyle reflect an application of his or her teachings?

In my early years as a pastor, I had great difficulty with people testing my authenticity. It frustrated me when I was asked, "Do you possess the Spirit?" or "Have you been born again?" or "Have you experienced 'this' or 'that' program?" Although I could answer the questions positively, I felt I was wasting time with explanations when we could be moving ahead. Not until an incident in Kansas City did I truly appreciate how necessary it is to test authenticity.

To reach Kansas City, I had flown halfway across the continent. A late arrival meant I had to eat on the run and rush to the convention where I gave three talks of a very intense nature. At the end of my final presentation, a woman I guessed to be in her mid-thirties came forward and asked, "Do you walk in the Spirit?"

Tired and wearing thin, I snapped, "I believe that when a person walks in the Spirit, others who also walk in the Spirit have no need to ask. They know."

The woman pulled back, her smile gone. "I . . . I'm sorry," she said. "But you see, I've just begun to walk in the Spirit and am still learning so much. Religion and prayer are all new to me, and I'm a bit scared. I'm trying hard to be sure I listen only to people who will be able to help me. I felt you were speaking just to me today, and I had to check it out."

Oh, to take back my brusque response! Drawing a deep breath, I apologized and explained what my day had been like. Then we talked at length about how it feels at the beginning of our journey. By the time our conversation ended, the woman was smiling again, and I had a better understanding of the importance of testing for authenticity.

Whenever we move into a new area of experience, our tendency is to look for people with similar experiences. Through sharing, we authenticate what has happened to us. Over the years I have discovered the importance of sharing more and more of my own journey. Other pilgrims can then compare their experiences with mine, and in a very real sense, test me to see if I am real from their point of view. At a conference I was conducting in Florida, I discovered that the teachers are not the only ones who get tested for authenticity.

This conference was attended mainly by medical professionals. After an all-morning session on spirituality, I asked the participants to spend some quiet time reviewing their lives and matching the stages of growth to their individual journeys. When we regathered later in the afternoon, a dentist from New York said, "I have another way of looking at the whole issue of testing authenticity." Although he acted hesitant, I sensed that he was overflowing with feelings he needed to express. With a little encouragement, he agreed to share his insights with the group. This is what Tom had to say:

> I don't know if I can verbalize what I want to, but I'm aware that I'm not testing the speaker's authenticity as much as I'm testing my own. This conference was recommended to me by a friend I trust, so I really didn't worry about you. I figured you were for real.

But now I find I'm measuring myself against you to see how authentic I am. If you are an example of what it means to be a person of prayer and open to the God-call to wholeness, then how am I in relation to you? Not that I have to be like you. But I have to know that someone is what I think I want to be, and that I can see within them some measure of what I want to be. I really am testing my own authenticity rather than testing yours. Yours is not an issue with me, but *my* authenticity is.

Tom's honest self-evaluation prompted me to caution him about the Christian competition game. Although we all need models for comparison, we are not out to become "better than" other Christians. For one brief conference I provided that model for Tom, and I feel certain that he is now a model for others.

As Christians we strive to follow Jesus, so it would be a mistake to turn responsibility for our spiritual growth over to any leader who might in effect become our messiah. We do, however, need role models who confirm our hopes that it is possible to become something more than we are.

I recall how Freida, a woman with whom I shared a spiritual director-directee relationship, discovered the part a role model played in her journey. One day she called and asked me a question. When I replied, "I don't really know," Freida quipped, "What! Ron DelBene doesn't have the answer?" There was a pause before she added, "Something significant just happened. I'll have to think about it and get back to you."

A few days later, Freida called back. She made some small talk before saying, "You're on the path too, aren't you?" I smiled to myself, reminded of my own moments of doubting, seeking, and receiving insights. "Yes, Freida," I said. "I, too, am on the path."

When Freida next spoke, her voice was warm with appreciation. "Well, thanks for letting me make you my messiah for a while," she said. "I never would have moved into the journey as I have if I hadn't thought you were altogether and finally finished. I guess I had to believe for a time that perfection was possible. Now, I think I can be on the journey with you."

As Freida discovered, it is helpful to have someone against whom to measure ourselves at certain points during our journey. Unfortunately, some people remain at this stage, spending a lifetime trying to be like someone else and constantly measuring themselves against that person. Some teachers, dealing with their own ego needs, encourage this dependency. The guideline is to accept help when we need it from those who can give it to us, but always to remember that no one of us has arrived spiritually. We are all travelers on a journey that takes us deeper into the life of the Spirit.

The Discipline Stage
"There is a positive side to discipline."

✳

Discipline has a negative connotation for most of us. The very word creates butterflies in the stomach and a tightness in the shoulders because it suggests a painful experience. For me, one such experience involved a second grade teacher I will call Miss Sutter who taught penmanship in a room where every wooden desk had an inkwell. I can still recall my tight grip on the pen and my fingers cramping as I painfully formed endless rows of A's , B's, C's, and on through all twenty-six letters of the alphabet. The result of Miss Sutter's demanding standards was that I, along with everyone else in her class, learned to write at least reasonably well.

Even though we may have unpleasant memories involving discipline, we know that no skill is acquired without being attentive to the learning process. If the word *discipline* calls forth negative feelings, I suggest substituting *attentiveness*. Being attentive is more than just paying attention. It means "to be faithful," and faithfulness is the key to discipline as it relates to our spiritual journey. We are called to be faithful people, and the idea of faithfulness is the theme of God's call to the Hebrew leaders as well as to the people themselves: "You shall be my people, and I will be your God" (Ezek. 36:28). Although the people did not remain faithful, God did not turn away from them. God's faithfulness is forever.

To be faithful means to submit to another or "to place oneself under another." When that kind of submission is linked with love, we are not a slave to the other but a friend (John 15:14-16). Discipleship, too, is related to this kind of submission in that, as a disciple, we place ourselves under the teaching of another. Disciple and discipline come from the same root word.

Disciples are *attentive* to the words and actions of the teacher. As Christ-followers, we are called to put on the mind of Jesus and place ourselves under the new law of love. Loving as Jesus loved lets people know we are his disciples. Jesus often refers to the "good and faithful servant" and reminds us that to be faithful and attentive is to be disciplined.

Examples of the disciplined life are all around us. People who run, and are faithful to running, come to a point at which they cease being people who run. They are runners. People who play the piano, and are faithful in their practice, at some point are no longer people who play. They are pianists. Likewise, people who pray, and are attentive and faithful in praying, reach a point at which they undergo a change. They are pray-ers, but more than that, they *are* prayer.

How much easier it would be if spiritual growth occurred as naturally as grass growing or trees budding in the spring. But we know it doesn't happen that way. Although we begin life as spiritual beings, growth demands effort on our part. Scripture tells us: "I know all about you: how you are neither cold nor hot. I wish you were one or the other, but since you are neither, but only lukewarm, I will spit you out of my mouth" (Rev. 3:15-16, JB).

Despite the call to go beyond the average—to be something more than lukewarm—many people do not respond. A Flemish writer on spiritual matters, Jan van Ruysbroeck, referred to Zaccheus as someone willing to go beyond the average. In his fourteenth century writings, van Ruysbroeck suggested that we must be like Zaccheus, who ran ahead of the crowd and climbed a tree so that he might see Jesus.

The problem with many people in the discipline stage is that they are not certain which tree to climb! They feel ambiguous. Although they recognize the need to be more attentive to their spiritual life, they see a forest ahead of them where each tree has a different sign: "Study," "Fast," "Minister," "Pray," and so on. Instead of climbing any one tree, people at this stage hold back, sure that some day they will recognize the ideal way to grow spiritually.

Barbara found not knowing which tree to climb to be a problem both in her professional and spiritual life. Throughout her seminary training, she felt called to serve in youth ministry. Once ordained she immediately found herself deeply involved with programs, planning, and people. Parents and teachers expected her to know what would "work" with young people. Barbara drove herself to become aware of new thinking and trends so that she could be on top of her job. Then came a day when she wondered what her wide-ranging attempts were accomplishing. This is what she confided in her journal:

It seems that the greatest difficulty with the students is that this week it's one approach and next week it's another. They're in it for the hype they can get. . . . And then I became aware that I didn't have anything concrete to give them either. I was just like they were. While I was in the seminary, there was a particular approach I used to develop my spiritual life. Then when I got out, I was involved with something else and have never settled into any form of discipline for myself.

When people stop jumping from method to method and program to program, they are more at peace. Whatever facet of spiritual development they pursue gets their full attention, and they soon reap the rewards of a more focused and disciplined life. I have found this to be especially true among people who give their faithful attention to prayer. I don't mean the rote praying of memorized prayers, although that type of prayer is important. The kind of prayer I am referring to is something we become. It is the faithful attitude that leads us to pray even when we don't feel like praying (Rom. 12:12). It is what we do in response to a God who is ever-faithful. This is positive discipline, and something Anthony found very difficult.

Anthony was an investment banker who at age thirty-six was a financial success, but found it difficult to be attentive to his spiritual needs in a regular, ever-deepening way. For several years he had been like a hungry child, heaping more on his spiritual plate than he could handle. He began a serious reading program, dropped it by the wayside, felt guilty, and then began the cycle all over again by trying something new. Finally he realized what was happening and considered a simpler approach. As he explained in his journal, focusing on prayer seemed a reasonable goal:

> I've been talking a good game for years about this religion stuff, but now I see prayer related to all areas of my life. I have been going to "get into" a discipline for a long time now. The idea of being faithful strikes me the most. I have a high regard for faithful people. Maybe it's time for me to be one.

What about you? Are you ready to see the positive side of discipline? Do you feel the desire to be more attentive to some aspect of your spiritual growth? If so, why not decide on an area and begin focusing on it now? Start with something at which you will experience success, remembering that you run a mile before you run a marathon.

CHAPTER 9

The Rebelling Stage

"I feel bored and want to give it all up . . ."

✳

After Elaine recognized that discipline could be a positive force in her life, she became more committed to her spiritual growth. Prayer was at the heart of the changes she experienced, and she was consistently attentive to it. At the time, she was in her mid-thirties and felt she was "on her way" spiritually. But all that changed abruptly as we see in one of her journal entries:

> I woke up one morning and thought, I bet there are 35,999 people in our town of 36,000 who are not going to get out of bed this morning to sit in prayer, read the scripture, and reflect upon God's Word. Then why am I? Who do I think I am? I mean, really, why do I think I am so special?

Because Elaine had been feeling so buoyed by her disciplined life, she was not prepared for the rebelling stage of her journey. Just as she began to appreciate the joy of her growth in faith, her resolve to be a faithful person was challenged.

As we enter this stage, there seems to be a tormentor inside us who is intent on raising doubts about the validity of our journey. It is as though we are approaching that moment of being all together and suddenly things come apart. The tormentor reflects a lifetime of doubts about our potential. It is the inner voice that has always reminded us of our shortcomings:

"You're not really smart."

"You're not really attractive."

"You're not really lovable."

"So of course, you're not really called to be holy."

The rebelling stage is that point on the journey where we may remember (sometimes in the most vivid detail) all our sinful actions. We are the star in a past that replays itself like a movie that portrays only our weaknesses, failures, and shortcomings. The message we receive is that our sins could never be totally forgiven, and that we could not be special to God.

At this stage in our journey, the teacher or the guide who had previously been so helpful may appear to have feet of clay and be unworthy of our confidence. We begin to look for faults in that person so we can justify saying there is nothing to all this religious stuff. Or we hedge by saying that if there is something to it, we can find the way ourselves.

Shannon reached the rebelling stage after she had already made several U-turns on her faith journey. Each time this happened, she had the confidence to continue seeking and persisted in her attempts to be attentive to her faith development. But when she got to the rebelling stage, she became depressed. This is what she entered in her journal:

I would describe this as a spiritual low point.
I feel tired and depressed and actually seem to
will not to pray. . . . Very uptight and tense. I am
empty. I feel just bored and want to give it all
up.

The rebellion stage is not a pleasant one to be in. Yet
despite the doubts and the despairing moments, it is a
positive part of the journey. How can this be? Because it
is the beginning of self-revelation, and our inner voice
urges caution for we are about to meet the person God
created us to be. That person has often been hidden from
view, and we are anxious about the discoveries we will
make. How understandable that we might want to back
off.

Hamilton was a lawyer who began to question his
journey and where it was taking him. Although he
thought of himself as rational and even-tempered, others
perceived him as unfeeling—something Hamilton was
not aware of. He was a highly disciplined person in all
areas of his life, so when he made up his mind to pray
regularly, he was faithful to his commitment. His breath
prayer, which formed the foundation of his prayer life,
was "Father, let me feel your love." Being the kind of person he was, Hamilton expected to see results.

After praying his prayer for about six months, Hamilton came to see me to talk over an uneasiness he felt
about his spiritual journey. To me it was obvious that
significant changes were taking place within him. I asked
how he was getting along at home and how he was relat-
ing to people at work.

"My wife mentioned something about my being more gentle, especially with the kids," Hamilton said. He went on to explain that the legal secretaries had talked about his being so pleasant that it seemed as if he were just back from a vacation. When I asked what he thought about these comments, Hamilton said, "I'm afraid people might take advantage of me if I'm too gentle or pleasant." A bit later in the conversation, he said, "The main reason I wanted to see you is that my breath prayer is beginning to change. I used to always say, 'Father, let me *feel* your love,' and now I'm saying, 'Father, let me *know* your love.' "

"What's the matter?" I asked. "Are you beginning to feel his love?"

Hamilton immediately caught my meaning. "Yeah, I guess so," he admitted, "but it's scary!"

Having opened himself to healing and wholeness, Hamilton was now having to deal with what had occurred: His prayer was being answered. He was becoming the even-tempered person he had believed himself to be but was not. His wife and the people at the office recognized the change even before he did. Hamilton found this to be scary. And no wonder, because it is. When wholesome, newly-discovered aspects of ourselves emerge, we often try to hold on to the familiar. What God asks of us is that we live into new growth and move on.

In my own journey, I experience the rebelling stage most often in those moments throughout the day when a window of time opens. It is those five or ten bonus minutes when an appointment is late, or when I arrive early for a meeting and am sitting in the car in the parking lot.

During those times I listen to this conversation in my head:

"Great, you've got this time to get some work done."

"Come on, intentionally take some time being aware of God's presence."

"But you could get one more thing done in these few minutes."

"Yes, and that one thing could be being attentive to God in silence for a minute or two."

And so it goes. I wish I could say that I always choose to take the time right then to be still and aware of what it means to be in God's presence. But after more than thirty years of trying to be attentive to God, there are still times when after having completed the "one more thing" with which I filled the window of time, I shrug my shoulders, smile to myself, and admit that it is a constant challenge to be faithful to a life of prayer.

In the rebelling stage the two greatest temptations are to go it alone or to drop out. Because it is difficult to admit our weaknesses to another person, the trap is set. Often we step right in and drop back to an earlier stage.

When we feel the rebel within, it is especially important to confide in someone who understands the pilgrim's way. Often we feel that we are in a static place, a place of no movement. The person in whom we confide may help us see that this is the point at which we are asked to continue reaffirming our dependence on God. Recognizing that we are dependent on God and not on ourselves is both a fearful and a freeing experience, and one against which we rebel.

Just as all the previous stages have been temporary, so too is the rebelling stage. Each time I am at this place on my journey, I recall something a friend shared with me: "Remember that, when shifting from low to high gear, you have to go through neutral."

CHAPTER 1 0

The Urged-On Stage

"Whatever it is that is moving me won't let me stop."

*

A friend of mine once had a car with a broken gas gauge. Because he was never sure how much gas was in the tank (especially after his children drove the car) he would find himself sputtering to a halt in the middle of an important trip. My friend's experience has an application to our spiritual journey. The urged-on stage is one in which we figuratively run out of gas and can go no further alone. In order to move on, we must have the help and encouragement of others.

Sam was at a point in his faith journey where he found himself stalled. He was a construction worker with a wife and four children and lived with a lot of stress. Layoffs, which are so common in his field, were a particular concern. Sam's faith life was a great source of comfort to him, but a time came when he began to neglect his spiritual growth. He described the experience this way:

> On the surface, each day seemed too busy for me to find time to pray. A week passed. What a loss! Looking back, I know I could have cut my lunch time short. But not praying on Saturday and Sunday was pure stubbornness on my part. My mind tried to convince me that I

didn't need to pray anymore. Nevertheless, my heart wanted to be aware of God's presence. My whole being yearned for the experience. I was driven to begin again.

In Sam's case, the Spirit was at work, urging him on when he could not continue alone. His experience reminds me of Psalm 42 in which the psalmist says:

> Why are you cast down, O my soul,
> and why are you disquieted within me?
> Hope in God; for I shall again praise him,
> my help and my God.
> Psalm 42:11

Like Sam, many of us will be urged on by the Spirit, but we may also benefit from the help of individuals and groups. Throughout the week we can have private time with God, whereas Sunday provides an opportunity to share our faith with others. In our churches, we and the other members of our faith community celebrate our faith and are urged to go forth and do God's work in the world.

Not all people, however, respond favorably to being urged on through communal celebration. A few are even antagonized by it. At one time or other, I suspect every member of the clergy has heard a variation of these remarks spoken to me by a parishioner. "I want you to know," she said sternly, "that I come to church on Sunday for my time with God. I come to worship, not to celebrate. And your celebration is getting in the way of my worship. Sunday is the only time I can really pray, and I want my time with God alone!"

I am never quite sure how to respond to such people. I don't think they want to understand that even though we may pray in private, prayer is a communal action. We are not saved as isolated individuals to enter a private kingdom of God; we are called in community and invited to the wedding banquet. I have noticed that people who want only to be alone with God often have small smiles, rarely laugh, and seem to be not only alone, but lonely. Their fierce independence sets them apart, and I wonder if they ever have the need to be urged on. Perhaps their beliefs are so fixed they never suffer from doubts, but I don't believe that to be the case.

In some churches, parishioners consider it solely the pastor's responsibility to do the urging. This is unfair for a number of reasons, but mainly because it deprives church members of an opportunity to share the Christian experience. When I was a pastor in a small Alabama town, I experienced what happens when parishioners assume responsibilities. They flower! They open up and share the beauty that God has placed within them.

As pastor of this parish, I saw how praying with and for one another during the week created a joyous unity that was apparent before, during, and after shared worship. Time and time again throughout my years of pastoring I have seen that people who have a common experience in Bible study or a weekend retreat or a social outreach project also have a great desire to celebrate in community. Through their celebration they encourage and support one another.

I see an analogy between what takes place in a loving faith community and a phenomenon that occurs in nature. When geese fly in formation, the lead position changes often. The lead goose drops back to the side where the air passes easily and another moves to the cutting edge of the formation. When one goose is hurt or weak and drops back, at least one other goose goes along. But for me the most fascinating aspect of all this is that geese honk encouragement from behind. They urge one another on.

On your spiritual journey, you may sometimes feel that you are not flying with the support of others, but are a solitary person going it alone. Even though it may seem that way, such is not the case. Others are also making the journey. They are, so to speak, "honking from behind," urging you on.

At times the lines separating the stages of spiritual growth blur. For instance, while feeling anxious and rebellious we might also be urged to move ahead. My good friend Bill is an example of this ambivalence. He is a doctor who has been on the journey for years, and through both the peaks and valleys of his life remains a faithful pilgrim. Here is one of his journal entries:

> I know why I cannot stop now. I've known for some time that whatever has been moving me in the direction I have been going in the last four years is more powerful than I am. Whatever is moving me won't let me stop. The pages continue to be turned and the pilgrim travels on.

The Confession Stage

"I had to stop, look honestly at these things,
and confess."

✳

Our entire journey is a process of putting off the old person and putting on the new (Eph. 4:22-24). Often along the path of that journey we recognize that we have sinned and try to make amends. But when we reach the confession stage, we view our sinfulness in much more detail. We see our past not through a glass darkly but clearly, perhaps even through a magnifying glass. When Jane reached this stage, she described her experience this way:

> All of a sudden it was like traveling down the highway and seeing my past on the billboards in front of me. I couldn't go on. I had to stop, look honestly at these things, and confess that I had sinned.

For some time, Jane had been aware of great changes in her spiritual life. What was happening reminded her of John the Baptist calling for repentance because the Kingdom of God was at hand (Matt. 3:2). When we experience that "at-handness," we know that the old has been—or is about to be—stripped away, and something new will take its place.

This experience of the new replacing the old calls to mind something that happened near our home. We live in a rural area, and a few miles away the interstate from Birmingham to Atlanta was under construction for several years. During that time, we saw the nearby mountains made low and the valleys brought up (Isa. 40:4). We watched the crooked old road made straight. This same process takes place in our spiritual lives. When we come to the confession stage and work our way through it, we feel more at ease on our journey, more balanced. God makes the mountains and valleys even. Crooked parts of our lives, which once made us afraid to see what was around the corner, are made straight.

In the confession stage, we look back. We reflect on how good God has been to us and feel humbled by our lack of appreciation. This is how Jane wrote about it:

> As I look more and more on the way that God has called me from so many places and brought me into his loving care and direction, I am overwhelmed that God would care for me.

Wrongdoings, which previously may have seemed inconsequential, now become significant. We feel compelled to make amends for those occasions when we believe we have sinned. Some of those sins are easily pinpointed: times when we lied, stole, or cheated. Others are not so easily recognized.

In Old English, *sin* is an archery term that means missing the target. As we progress along the pilgrim's way, we become much more aware of the target that is God's love. All those times we have missed the target can leave us with an accumulated sense of failure and feelings of sinfulness that aren't so easily identified.

The recognition that we need to set things right—need to confess our sins—may be the most painful part of our journey. So painful, in fact, that we try to avoid it. Frequently people backtrack from this stage, putting off that which we are called to do. What they fail to appreciate is that God's love and mercy are boundless. No scripture lets us know this more surely than the story of the prodigal child who returns home to the welcoming parent (Luke 15:11-32). God is such a parent, waiting to enfold us with warmth and forgiveness.

How we seek forgiveness is an individual matter. You may prefer to do it privately with Jesus as your guide, remembering that:

> If anyone does sin, we have an advocate with the Father, Jesus Christ the righteous; and he is the atoning sacrifice for our sins, and not for ours only but also for the sins of the whole world.
>
> 1 John 2:1-2

You may, however, find it consoling to seek forgiveness with the help of another person through the ritual of "confessing" or "making yourself whole before God." As part of my ministry, sharing those issues of life which people consider sin is a humbling experience. For me it is a great gift to know that someone is willing to put aside the old and put on the new in the presence of God and me as God's minister. Often it is with fear and trepidation that someone asks me to "hear my confession before God." The fact that I can act in the name of the community of believers and that God has given that power (John 20:22-23) is an immense relief to those who seek forgiveness in this way. It is a profound experience to have a hand placed upon your head and to hear that you are forgiven. Indeed, touch is often more healing than words.

At this point, I want to stress that the confession stage is a call to do more than seek forgiveness for a particular sin. It is a call to radically alter not just a part of your life but your whole life, to look at yourself and see what causes you to miss the mark. To accomplish this, I recommend a life review. This will take no more than an hour, and in the process, you are likely to discover a pattern of turning away from God's love.

To do a life review you need pencil and paper and a quiet place where you are assured of privacy. Then follow these simple steps:

1. Sit in a comfortable position and take two or three deep breaths to relax yourself.

2. Pray the Lord's Prayer or read a favorite passage from Scripture. Psalm 139 is appropriate.

3. List those instances when you consciously chose to miss the mark as a child of God. Either begin in the present and go back year by year, or begin with your earliest memories and move forward. It is not necessary to go into elaborate detail, nor to relive the experiences. Your list is a way to focus on your life experiences up to the present. (If other people are involved, do not name them. In the event the list is lost, their privacy would be violated.)

Sally set out to do a life review, and only part of the way through her list she had this insight:

> The more I remembered, the more aware I became of a pattern in my life. It seems that I was always motivated by envy. And I think that envy has really been the basic issue with me since a very young age.

Envy had led Sally to sin in many ways, but it is doubtful she would have understood this without making the list and seeing a pattern of behavior. Her life review gave her the information she needed to make a basic change that would affect all areas of her life.

Paul, too, had an insight while doing his life review. At thirty-eight, he was a busy husband and father of two children who was more concerned about others than about himself. After doing a life review, he described his new awareness this way:

> I must reorder my entire life. I need to get out of debt and free myself of a terrible burden. I need to practice seeing Jesus in everyone. I need to care for my body with diet and exercise. I need to do more praying. I need to bridle my anger. How long this enormous struggle within me will go on, I don't know. It's like washing out a stubborn stain. I became aware of the truth. I must change.

Once you have made your list, you can put it to use in several ways. Some people find it helpful to go alone into a quiet church and take the time to read through the list and turn it over to God. Still others do the same thing in the privacy of their home. Of course you can also use your list as you seek forgiveness in the presence of a priest, minister, or friend who understands your need for verbalizing your confession. After asking for and accepting forgiveness, throwing away or burning the list can be a symbolic act that reinforces your resolve to be a new person.

Whatever you choose to do at this stage, remember that forgiveness is a healing process and that you are being called to a new place. In a journal entry, Janet expressed how she felt about this:

> I have irrevocably turned from my past world view and, as I have turned, I don't know where I am. I leave behind the old world of certainties, and turn to the world of uncertainties...
>
> I feel myself creating each new moment and each situation. I do not know where I am. I am happy, but I don't know where to turn. I am between two worlds.

Feeling that we are standing between two worlds can be painful. Although we are relieved at having confessed, we experience both great uncertainty and great expectancy. Like Janet, we may feel that something worth waiting for is going to happen, but we have no idea what it is.

For many pilgrims this stage is one of great loneliness. In their writings they liken it to a torturous desert where they see only sand and more sand and have no sense of direction. This leads to painful uncertainty, especially for those who have a need to feel in control of their lives. The stage is temporarily a sand trap, a place they want desperately to get out of.

Carol felt the pain of the confession stage so intensely that she called me long distance. "I *know* there's something around the corner," she said, "and I'm moving toward it, but I can't see it! I just feel alone!" She cried briefly, then composed herself enough to ask, "Why is it always so painful to move into a new place?"

Although I wasn't able to explain it as well as I wanted to on the phone, Carol seemed to understand that she would not be stalled at this difficult place forever. She accepted that her confusion and uncertainty were temporary, and that one day she would know that this was part of the process of her journey. A follow-up conversation revealed that soon after talking to me she had, indeed, moved through the pain and on to another stage.

Identifying and verbalizing our sin may bring about a shift of consciousness, which in turn results in a shift of focus. That is, we move from *focusing on the pain that growth involves to focusing on the growth that results from moving through the pain.* This is a subtle but important point. Along the pilgrim's way we all experience "desert times." Some of these times include loneliness or pain or both. While we are going through these experiences, they may seem senseless, but insight will come with time. By confessing our sins we outwardly express a part of ourselves that is transformed by God's power and love.

CHAPTER 12

The Insight Stage

"Oh, now I see. . . ."

✳

At some point in our journey there is a fleeting time when an insight leads us to say, "That's it!" or "Aha!" or "Oh, now I see." Often it occurs so suddenly that we are at a loss to talk about it, or will do so only after a bit of reflection. The insight serves as a reminder that we can always be surprised by God.

To the person experiencing the insight stage, the revelation has a deep, personal meaning. The insight may not, however, seem all that important to others, and the called-for change might be considered insignificant. But when the insight is our own, the experience is crucial. It tells us that radical change has to take place before we can proceed on the journey of spiritual growth.

For Jason, a brash, self-centered young man, this stage led him into a time of reflection about his true self. This excerpt from his journal explains what happened:

> I began to see clearly that it was not that I wasn't loving and attentive to people, but that I wasn't always aware of them. I guess because of my natural ability to be friendly, people didn't notice that I wasn't always "present" to them. Now I'm more attentive, and that's a radical

change for me. I don't know what I expected at this stage, but what I got surely is the answer for me.

Jason was coming to realize what the apostle Paul means when he talks about being transformed by the renewing of our minds (Rom. 12:2). At the insight stage we discover a new person emerging. It is a surprise to look in the mirror and see the same face and same body, because we *know* the interior has been radically changed. Interestingly, the change is usually not at all what we expected.

People who have been at the previous stage (confession) for some time tend to build up unrealistic expectations for what is to come. They anticipate a kind of flashy Hollywood production full of special effects. Imaginary scenarios are created around such questions as:

• What should I be doing?
• What should God be doing for me?
• Who should be leading me?

The ego builds up improbable images of what we think we *should* experience. But instead of a starring role in a major production, we are likely to discover that what God has in mind is more akin to being in a home video! Although this can be disappointing, I seldom find that to be the case. Rather, the insight stage is a humbling experience wherein we realize that most people don't seek first the kingdom of God; they seek first *their place* in the kingdom. The "Aha!" comes about when we truly accept that God's kingdom is given to us, and that we have no need to worry about our place in it.

The "Aha!" came to Donna after she had spent many years working in church and social ministries. Although her work was appreciated, she was active in so many areas that no one recognized her as an expert or specialist in any one thing. When Donna reached her forties, she felt a restlessness that she interpreted as a call to focus her work in a particular area. Here she describes what happened to her at the insight stage:

> I suddenly saw all my life as ministry, and it had nothing really to do with church or social issues or other people. Instead I saw my ministry as a well of living water within me just bubbling and overflowing. It was no longer a question of "What ministry?" It became a realization that *my life is ministry!* Oh, how dumb I am! Why didn't I see that this was the answer all along?

Insights often leave us feeling dumb, foolish, or embarrassed, because we believe we "should have known that" at our age or with our experience. Perhaps we did know it, but for some reason ignored the obvious. Finally God makes it clear. In Donna's case she came to realize that ministry is not only something you do, it is something you are. Jesus himself *was* ministry. Jesus' whole mission is to make God known and to transfer God's life to us (John 17:1-4).

Although we pass through each of the stages many times, the insight stage always stands out. Perhaps you have heard it described as a "peak" or "mountaintop" experience. Many such experiences are recorded in the Bible. I do not think our experiences are so different from Peter's mountaintop experience at the transfiguration.

Matthew's account shows Peter talking about wanting to preserve what happened. While Peter is still talking, he is interrupted by God in the bright cloud that envelops them (Matt. 17:1-8).

How often we are like that! We get so busy trying to package and preserve our religious past that God has to interrupt us and make things cloudy. Only upon reflection can we see the brightness of the insight and what God has revealed to us.

So far we have seen how the stages not only lead one into the other but also provide the opportunity to stay where we are, or even move back to where we believe we will be more secure. It is tempting to think of the insight stage as a satisfactory end point when, in fact, the growth we can experience in our relationship with God is endless. Certainly the insight is to be enjoyed, and we don't always have to be "getting somewhere else." But where we are is not where we will always be. More surprises await us.

The insight stage is a good time to look anew at what we expect from our prayers. Many people come to prayer hoping to repeat an experience. I suggest coming to prayer with the attitude that your experience will be entirely new. Let it be a time of thankfulness for what has happened and a time to open yourself to being stretched beyond where you are.

As you look back on your spiritual life, you will recall moments when you experienced a revelation that made you smile and say, "Oh, now I see." That was an awareness of God's time and your time intersecting in a joyful and humbling moment. Celebrate those moments, and be assured they will occur again.

The Release Stage

"I am giving my power over to God in everyday practical things."

✳

Frank was a private person who always reminded me of the lone, independent cowboy determined to be in charge of his own destiny. Although he was a fighter, Frank was slowly dying, and there was nothing he could do about it. For one of the first times in his life, he was not in charge.

Soon Frank would be passing over to the risen life. Despite his faith in God, I knew these final moments were extremely difficult for him. He was not accustomed to giving his power over to anyone, and his struggle was evident to those of us who visited him in the hospital. Finally the time seemed right, and I asked Frank's family if I could be alone with him. They agreed.

With just the two of us in the room, I bent close to Frank and asked if he could hear me. He nodded but did not open his eyes. "Frank," I said very gently, "one of these times will be the last time we talk together. I want you to know how much it has meant to me to know you." Frank opened his eyes and looked directly at me. Previously we had talked a lot about his illness. Many times he had told me how tired he was of the pain and of being sick. Now he didn't say a word.

"You have always been a fighter," I said, "but there may come a time soon when you just don't think you can fight any longer. You need to know it's OK to release your power to God and go with Jesus. He will come to you as he has in your dreams. When he does, just take his hand and enter into the peace of his loving."

Frank nodded and closed his eyes. "Thanks," he murmured. "Peace. . . ." Then he smiled faintly, and I left his room.

To the very end, Frank was stubborn about releasing his grip on power. This is not surprising considering that, as Americans, we pride ourselves on a history of rugged individualism. The very idea of opening ourselves to another's loving power suggests weakness and inability. This is an unfortunate attitude, because the release-of-power stage of our spiritual journey represents something quite different. Rather than revealing weakness and inability, the release stage demonstrates strength and ability.

Releasing our controlling grip on power and experiencing God's creative power inspires a feeling of awe. In that regard it is similar to the confession stage in which we are aware of how wondrous God is and how sinful we have been. Overwhelmed by God's love for us, and the fact that we have done nothing to earn that love, we focus on confession. In the release stage we focus on awe. Awe comes from understanding that although we appear insignificant, God is most gracious to us.

Ellen was a young teacher dealing with issues of control. Still at that point in her career where she felt threatened by the children's potential to disrupt her classroom, she feared turning too much control over to them.

Some of this same concern about control spilled over into her spiritual life. This is what Ellen wrote in her journal:

> This whole area of giving my power over was a confusing one to me. But last week I had that tremendous awareness of the "Aha!" in my life. It was as if I was plunged into a pool that was clear and reflecting; the kind in which you can see the whole of the trees on the shore and the sky and sun reflected. Well, I was the pool and I saw the reflection of God in me. . . . It's a strange feeling, because if God were not there I would have nothing to reflect. But also, if I were not here and open to be aware of it, there would be no reflection of God in this place. Maybe that's what the Psalms mean by the "fear of the Lord."

At some point in our lives, most of us probably think of the fear of the Lord as "dread" or "terror." As we mature spiritually we are better able to see this fear as Ellen saw it—an awesomeness that God intends us to reflect!

I once spent over six months at the release stage and moved on only after an experience that left me awed by the love that is God. I had flown to Denver, Colorado, to see a friend who lived in the mountains outside the city. When we arrived at his home around midnight, there wasn't much to see. The following morning I got up early to pray and slipped quietly downstairs to the living room. When I reached the bottom of the stairs, I felt as if I was still on a plane. Directly ahead of me, outside the glass wall, was a huge mountain. Sunlight made it look like a crystal rainbow. It was one of those larger-than-life experiences that takes your breath away.

In that instant I had a sense of what it is to be in fear of the Lord; to be in awe of the love that is God. And I asked myself, *Who am I? What significance do I have? What right do I have to exist in the presence of such majesty?* Yet I knew that I was special, as is every person God ever created. If we call to mind that without grains of sand there would be no beach, we realize that our seeming insignificance makes us significant.

Standing there watching the early morning light bathe the mountain landscape, I released my compulsive need for control to God. As I did so, this scripture rang in my ears:

> Those who trust in the Lord are like Mount Zion,
> which cannot be shaken but stands fast for ever.
> As the hills enfold Jerusalem,
> so the Lord enfolds his people, now and evermore.
> Psalm 125:1-2, NEB

Each time we pass through the release stage, we die to some part of ourselves that stubbornly wants to be in control and prevents us from understanding our true relationship to God. In these times of resistance, it helps to remember that even Jesus released his need to control into God's loving power.

A highly successful young lawyer I know understands how necessary it is to release the need for power. Professionally he enjoys considerable power and finds it important to take time to keep his life in perspective. After reviewing his experiences in the release stage, he made this entry in his journal:

> The implications of giving my power over are daily, I have discovered. It seems that I have become aware, time and time again, that I can give up some of my need to control. And I discover that this places me in a position of waiting again. I know that something is going to happen. I just don't know when.
>
> So I went to the woods today and again was aware of how awesome my God is. This is really a stage of growth that I can reflect upon and see that, in fact, I am giving my power over to God in everyday practical things.

What about you? Do you find yourself trying to go it alone and be in charge? Or are your senses open to hear the call to release your need for ultimate control so that God might more readily be reflected in what you say and do?

The Expectation Stage

"I know that it will happen, but I really don't know when."

✳

The temperature was in the high eighties, and the humidity seemed even higher as a group of friends and I stood outside the church talking. When Paul, a fellow parishioner, pulled his car up close to the sidewalk, we all turned to watch. His wife Pam was already a week overdue with their first child, and as she struggled to get out of the car, her discomfort was obvious. But with humor in her voice she turned to us and quipped, "Please pray for deliverance for me!"

Pam was at the "but when?" stage of her pregnancy, certain her child would be born soon, but not knowing exactly when. A comparison can be made between Pam's experience with pregnancy and the expectation stage of our spiritual journey. This stage is also a period of waiting during which we experience discomfort. Mostly, though, it is a period of hope because we know for certain that something new is coming into our life.

Each time I am at this stage and glance in a mirror, I see something different about myself. Perhaps no one else sees it, but I am reminded of that old saying, "You look like the cat that just swallowed the canary!" Pleased. Satisfied. Full. The words help explain my experience, but do not adequately express my feelings. Perhaps this line from the Psalms most surely reflects what it is like to be in the expectation stage: "Truly my heart waits silently for God" (Psalm 62:5, NEB).

Jim was married, happy with his life, and passing from one stage to another with a rapidity I do not often see. In his journal, he expressed the expectation stage with clarity:

> Now I guess the question is, "but when will this happen?" I see that I have moved along a particular path, and I find myself out of control. It's as if I have to sit and wait until it happens. I feel what it must be like being pregnant and knowing that the time is near, but not really knowing when. You keep looking for the signs, and even make them up and make them into more than they are. Is this the way it is supposed to be? Is this what Peter was experiencing when he always seemed to be a jump ahead of Jesus in what was supposed to happen? I guess I really can enjoy this time of waiting before God.

Although Jim passed quickly through many of the stages, other pilgrims find their journey quite different. At forty-three, Janet was a successful therapist who felt herself moving slowly, but definitely moving. Though she was extremely busy in her practice, she took time to journal, and over a period of three years shared her writings with me. This entry reflects the cycling and re-cycling of the stages from the point of view of someone at the expectation stage:

Is it forever that I have been waiting for all of this to come together? Each time I pray, I remind myself that I pray not to achieve anything but to be faithful in responding to God. . . . I see that it doesn't matter if I want to pray or not any more than it matters if I want to breathe. I will because I have chosen to respond to God's call for me.... Even though I have recalled times in the past when I have thought, "this time too shall pass and I will move into getting it all together," still it is waiting and asking, "When, O Lord, but when?"

At this point in our journey, we are confronted with a tremendous urge to control time. How we would like to rush time. How we would like to have more of it. How we misuse the time we do have.

I can recall the exact moment I decided it was not worth living my life on a tight schedule. Years ago I had a job that involved traveling by air about sixty percent of the time. I would land in a city and within an hour have rented a car and driven downtown for a meeting. I was not alone in this experience. In the business world, thousands of people travel this way each day, often making two or more cities in a twenty-four hour period.

One day as I was sitting in O'Hare airport in Chicago, I heard racing footsteps. I looked up and saw a man who was running hard, obviously trying to make his flight. He had an attaché case in his hand and a suit carryon flung over his shoulder. Because of the many times I, too, had raced to catch a plane, I identified with this man. Those times when I didn't make my connection, I often lost whole days that somehow had to be made up.

As the man got to the ticket counter near me, he gasped for breath and asked, "Did the plane for L.A. leave yet?"

"No," the agent said, "you still have time."

The man sighed and slapped his side. "Great! I made it!" Then he grabbed at his chest and slumped to the floor. He was dead.

That day I decided that living on such a tight schedule was not worth it. From then on, I began to see that all of time is sacred, not just those moments that fit our schedules. I have learned to move more gently with time. Now I work *with* it instead of *against* it, and I enjoy the moments I used to waste.

In so many areas of our lives we try to hurry up time and get on with the action. One of the important things we learn during the expectation stage is to appreciate the moments of waiting. In his journal, a young runner named Edward brings the various sensations of this stage into focus:

> It's like running in a race for me. This stage of asking "but when?" is like a certain point in a race. I begin to sense that it's all going to come out well. I feel scattered and anxious; I know that it will happen, but I really don't know when. . . .

The hope of this stage is certain to be fulfilled, because in spiritual labor, as in pregnancy, something new is entering our life. This does not happen according to our schedule, but will come about in due time.

The Integration Stage

"I have come to be comfortable with myself. . . ."

✳

How can we capture what it means when suddenly we recognize that life is coming together for us? Over time we have been going through the stages and laying the groundwork. Then comes that moment when all the tell-tale signs of the birthing have taken place and we look at what has happened within us. What we see is a new creation. Hard as it is to believe, this potential was within us all along, being nurtured and growing. Now is the time for it to become real and tangible outside ourselves.

For me, awareness of this integration occurs in the latter part of the expectation stage. Again and again, I get hints that the time is near. These hints might be likened to mild labor pains at first, then hard contractions. Usually confirmation that this is indeed the awaited moment comes from someone else. But for my wife, Eleanor, the confirmation seems to come from within. Frequently she experiences these times while out running and returns to the house wearing a knowing smile. Then she goes directly to her journal and I know that I must wait until that entry is made before I hear her tale of discovery. Often I feel I have to work hard to get my answers, while all she has to do is go out and run! Although I tell others that everyone receives insights in different ways, it took me a long time to accept the truth of this in my own life.

Many people expect this stage of the journey to be dramatic—maybe something comparable to a burst of fireworks in a night sky or the intensity of a full orchestra. Sometimes it is like that. But more likely it will be a quiet realization such as the one Susan, a young actress and director, expressed in her journal:

> Having everything come together like this while I have someone with whom to talk is great. I suspect that I wouldn't really reflect on these things if I were alone. I expected some great Broadway production finale when actually it happened rather quietly and deeply within. Beautiful.

For Susan, and for many others, the integration happens as if hands are laid upon their eyes and the scales fall away, letting them see anew. This is the type of experience we celebrate when we sing, "I once was lost, but now am found, was blind, but now I see."

Because integrating experiences tend to be preceded by times of waiting and quiet, people have difficulty pinpointing them. Also, we become impatient with waiting, and instead of persevering the full time, we return to a previous stage. Then we find ourselves saying, "You know, it seems as if I've been at this point many times before." Well, of course we have! Each time our impatience hinders the integration, we move into one of the former stages where we have already been.

Think about your own journey and look carefully at those times when you wanted to give up and say, "It's not worth it" or "It will never happen to me." Now you see how important it is to have patience and wait out the discouragement with prayer and a calm spirit.

Scripture tells us we are called to be perfect as God is perfect. As we discussed earlier, the word *perfect* as it is used in this context means together or integrated or whole. This puts perfection within reach; it is possible to be whole and at peace. Marian, a forty-two-year-old woman, tells how this stage of her journey involved developing a sense of self-worth. In her journal she wrote:

> How can I describe "knowing" that I am loved and having my life come together like this? Everything from the past week has pointed to this, yet I didn't see it all fall into place until this morning. The dreams that I have been having, the insights, were part of this great "getting it together. . . ."
>
> I have come to be comfortable with myself for the first time I can ever remember. I guess the secret is that I love me, and it doesn't really matter who else does.

The integration stage can be likened to putting the last piece of a jigsaw puzzle in place. When we see the entire picture of our journey, we have a sense of accomplishment and feel complete. We then understand that all along the way we were being prepared for wholeness.

Naturally we want this unifying experience to last forever. We want to always feel integrated and whole, but this stage is not eternal in the sense that we arrive and stay there a lifetime. We will have integrating experiences such as this throughout our life, and each time it will be as if another plant has bloomed in our garden, or another room has been added to our house.

Often roadblocks to feeling whole have roots in our childhood. This was true for Don, who had been involved in many high-powered renewal movements. He recorded this insight in his journal:

> After thirty-three years, I see clearly that the emotions which resulted from my previous encounters with God were so strong because I always wanted to be touched by my father as an act of acknowledgment and love. Then the thought came to me that perhaps Jesus was telling me I would feel his presence if I would first feel my own true presence.

Seeing a connection with childhood as Don did, or identifying another experience from our past, can open us to a peace never felt before. We can also open up to this peace by identifying some persistent or recurring need or truth about ourselves. Yet often we are reluctant to face those things that strike at the heart of us. The story of the woman at the well effectively points this out. When the Samaritan woman came to draw water, Jesus engaged her in conversation (John 4:5-30). Each time he revealed more to her about her life, or answered a deep yet unfulfilled need, she experienced a greater understanding of herself and continued to open like a bud come to bloom. How like her we are!

In helping people with their spiritual direction, I am amazed—and often in grace-filled awe—to see how

God's revealing power brings light and truth out of the dark places of their lives. I might ask, "Can you remember another time when you felt like this?"

There is usually a long, thoughtful pause before the person says, "Yes, I remember feeling like this not only one time but many times. Maybe there's a key to understanding this after all!"

At other times questions are met with great hesitation, even avoidance. For whatever reason, often because it is not yet time, we detour around learning the truth about our lives. But when we seek in honesty (perhaps with the help of a guide) the truth emerges. The discovery may amaze us, and like the Samaritan woman, we rush about saying, "Wait until I tell you what I discovered about myself!"

The surprising response we often get is, "I'm glad you finally saw that!"

At one point in my life I was eagerly awaiting an integrating moment of insight and peace. I was a young man anxious to find answers when I heard that Father P., a professor from India, was a wise spiritual guide. At the time he lived in California and I was living in Florida. When a business trip took me to California, I decided to stay an extra day and rent a car to go see him. I wrote for an appointment, and his secretary responded, saying he could meet with me at four on the day I suggested and that I was invited to stay for dinner. Needless to say, I was overjoyed.

After driving for two hours, I arrived at the scheduled time only to find that Father P. was not home. A guest at the house who spoke virtually no English (and I knew nothing of his east Indian dialect) greeted me at the door and invited me in.

The house guest and I sat in semi-silence for two hours. During this time I became restless, then annoyed. *Who did Father P. think he was to keep me waiting like this? After I had made such an effort to be here, he should be able to keep his appointment.*

An hour and a half after I arrived, Father P. whisked into the room. With a few brief words of apology, he ushered me into his library and seated himself behind a large desk. He invited me to take a chair in front of the desk. Then he said, "Begin."

Begin I did. For two hours I emptied myself to this man, telling him everything I felt he needed to know in order to give me the ultimate answer. When I finished, he got up and came from behind the desk. Taking a chair, he put it in front of me and sat so close our knees were touching. "Now," he directed, "pay attention."

My heart drummed and my mouth went dry. I was certain he was going to touch my forehead or my heart. Then instant sanctity, or at least enlightenment, would be mine. He leaned forward as if to touch me, and I held my breath. This was it! Like a gentle, loving grandfather, he pointed his right index finger at me and said, "Pray unceasingly, go home, love your wife and children, and do what needs to be done. Now let's go eat!" Rising abruptly, he led me to the dining room.

Stunned, I followed along. *For this advice—this enlightenment—I had gone to so much trouble?* I sat at the table feeling angry, tired, annoyed, confused. Throughout the meal Father P. conversed sporadically with his house guest in a language foreign to me. After taking my leave and making the two-hour drive to my hotel, I wanted to write what I was feeling and thinking but was unable to do so.

Back home the next day, I told Eleanor every detail of the story. When I finished, her gaze held fast to mine as she said, "Thank God someone finally told you that!"

Sometimes we are the last ones to know the truth about ourselves. I see now that this wise man's advice was one of the great coming-together moments of my life. His words were right for me, and I find that with a bit of adaptation they can be applied to anyone's life. Whatever our age or circumstance, we can pray and we can love. And when we do that, we will be growing spiritually and getting on with what needs to be done.

CHAPTER 16

Going On

"Each journey is both the same and different. . . ."

✳

And so, we come to the end. The end, however, is not the end, because after experiencing a time of wholeness we find ourselves moving once more through the awakening and seeking stages of the spiritual journey. Each journey is both the same and different: the same because we will once again be covering familiar ground while seeking or experiencing doubts or wondering what's coming. Yet it is different because we now have a history against which to compare and contrast what happens to us.

The original awakening that leads to a greater concern about spiritual growth is like a stone dropped into the water of our life. The first few ripples are very distinct, but as they move farther and farther out they become less distinguishable. Nevertheless, the ripples are still there. So it is as we pass through the stages time and time again. The earlier passings may dim, but the impressions remain.

Arthur was in his mid-thirties and had grown up with the idea that religion should be as steadfast and unyielding as a rock. He liked to think that once you reach a certain stage of spiritual growth you are complete and should be happy just to rest there. However, when he examined his attentiveness to God in more detail, he discovered that spirituality is not static, but rather something that is always changing and growing. Arthur reflected on this in his journal:

> It is helpful to understand that I have recycled—passed through the stages again—at least twice and am able to accept that. I have had feelings of guilt and anger for not staying in one place and have felt as if I was backsliding. Now I know it's not backsliding, it's simply integrating experiences at deeper levels and then going on.

Arthur's concern about backsliding is common. In the early months and years of spiritual growth, pilgrims on the way fail to realize that the principle of one-step-forward, two-steps-back does not apply. Even when we choose to remain where we are, or return to a more secure place, we are still in a movement toward God. Bear in mind that spiritual growth is not like climbing a ladder, but rather can be likened to the growth rings of a tree. With us, as with trees, growth varies from year to year.

What looks like backsliding often appears in retrospect to have been a necessary preparation for more complete understanding. Remember Peter's denial on the eve of the crucifixion (Luke 22:54-62). At first glance it would seem to be a step backward, but in the total picture Peter moves into a deeper commitment when Jesus asked, "Do you love me?" (John 21:15-17). The fact that Jesus asks the question three times undoubtedly heightens Peter's awareness of the times he declared his love for

Jesus, and then denied him. The depth of Peter's sorrow over the denial was probably surpassed only by the love he felt when Jesus said, "Feed my sheep" (John 21:17).

Likewise Paul's witnessing the death of Stephen and working to destroy the church seemed to be a step backward on his personal journey (Acts 7:58–8:3). Instead it was another step for Paul along the way to the Damascus road experience (Acts 9:1-6).

All our experiences provide fertile ground for God to plant seeds of faith and bring forth new fruit. Our growth with God, in turn, becomes ministry to others. We see this clearly in the examples of Peter and Paul. From their own failings came insights on the importance and focus of their ministry. We are like them. Our prayer life and spiritual growth will lead us to a greater understanding of our role in ministering to others, whether it be in our families, our work, our neighborhood or the wider world.

I find that those people who most yearn for God often have the greatest feelings of failure. Many people do not believe that God loves them unconditionally, so in order to be worthy of that love, they set difficult to impossible goals—goals they feel they must attain to be worthy of God's love. When they do not reach the goals, they see only their failure, their backsliding. It does not occur to them that the strivings themselves make the ground more fertile for the seeds of new life and ministry.

At fifty-eight, Robert was an architect with many clients and a very busy life that included a family of grown children. Although he had been attentive to his spiritual life, he had not found anything to help him make sense out of what he saw as a hodgepodge of experiences. Understanding that there were stages that could be passed through over and over gave him a practical way to make sense of his life's path. In his journal he wrote:

> In all areas of my life I am at different places in the stages of growth: at home with my family, at the office, in my life plans, in my inner life of prayer. No wonder I'm feeling scattered. I guess the best thing to do is . . . place my priorities where I need to in order to get all the areas in the same general place on my journey.

The stages of spiritual growth serve each of us in a somewhat different way. They are first of all guidelines to help make sense out of the yearnings, the doubts, the anger, and the wonder that enter every Christian's life. The stages are also a means of helping us see where we are today, where we were yesterday, and where we hope to be tomorrow. Most of all, the stages help us appreciate that there is no particular place we must "get to"; there is only a life to live. God calls us to wholeness, to live as Jesus lived, and to love as Jesus loved. As we earnestly strive to do that, we find that the hunger of the heart is satisfied.

The Breath Prayer

＊

Prayer is the cornerstone of spiritual life. Among the many forms of prayer is one known as the breath prayer. This prayer takes its name from the Hebrew word *ruach*, which can be translated as "wind," "breath," or "spirit." The *ruach* of God hovered over the waters of chaos in creation (Gen. 1:2) and God breathed the breath of life into all living beings (Gen. 2:7). Because this way of praying reminds us that we share God's breath, and because it comes as easily and naturally as breathing, it is known as the breath prayer.

This ancient form of prayer is found in writings as early as the second century. Perhaps the best known breath prayer is the one called the Jesus Prayer: "Lord Jesus Christ, Son of God, have mercy on me, a sinner." The Jesus Prayer originated in the Christian tradition of the East and can be traced back to the sixth century. At that time, monks and others who were seeking a deeper relationship with God sought a disciplined form of prayer they could pray anywhere and at anytime. This brief prayer encompassed all one needed to believe in order to be saved. Over time the Jesus Prayer was abbreviated to "Lord Jesus Christ, have mercy," and even "Jesus, mercy."

The approach to the breath prayer I suggest is like those ancient prayers of praise and petition that have been such an integral part of our Christian tradition. But instead of using other people's words, we each discover our own breath prayer. This prayer, which arises from our deepest need, gives us a way to follow the apostle Paul's admonishment to "pray without ceasing" (1 Thess. 5:17). Just as breathing supports life and renews our physical body, unceasing prayer keeps us attentive to God's presence and renews our spirit. To discover your breath prayer, follow these simple steps:

Step 1

Sit comfortably and calm yourself. Close your eyes and be mindful that you are in God's loving presence. Recall a passage from scripture that places you in a peaceful frame of mind. "Be still, and know that I am God!" (Psalm 46:10) is scripture that many people find calming.

Step 2

With your eyes still closed, imagine that God is calling you by name. Hear God asking: "(*Your name*), what do you want?"

Step 3

Answer God directly with whatever comes honestly from your heart. Your answer may be no more than a single word, such as *peace* or *love* or *forgiveness*. Your answer might instead be a phrase or a brief sentence, such as "I want to feel your forgiveness" or "I want to know your love." Whatever your response, it will be at the heart of your prayer.

Step 4

Choose your favorite name or image for God. Choices people commonly make include God, Shepherd, Jesus, Spirit, Living Fire, Creator, Lord, Christ, Eternal Light.

Step 5

Combine your name for God with your answer to God's question "What do you want?" and you have your prayer. For example:

What I want	Name I call God	Possible prayer
rest	Shepherd	My Shepherd, let me rest in thee.
to be led	Eternal Light	Lead me on my way, Eternal Light.
love	Jesus	Jesus, let me feel your love.

If several ideas occur, write down the various possibilities and then eliminate and/or combine ideas until you have focused your prayer. You may "want" many things, but wants can be narrowed to your deepest yearning that is basic to your spiritual well-being. The question to be asked is *What do I want that will make me feel most whole?* When you achieve a feeling of wholeness, serenity will deepen and flow into all areas of your life.

Once you get at the heart of your yearning, search for words that give it expression. Then work with these words until you have a prayer of six to eight syllables that flows smoothly when spoken aloud or expressed silently as heart thoughts.

Some prayers are most rhythmic when God's name is placed at the beginning. Others require it at the end. When your prayer seems right for you, use it again and again throughout the day. In time it will come as easily and naturally as breathing, and you will be answering scripture's call to pray unceasingly.

For a more in-depth look at prayer, and this form of prayer in particular, refer to my book, *The Breath of Life: A Simple Way to Pray*, published by Upper Room Books.

ABOUT THE AUTHORS

The Rev. Ron DelBene holds a master's degree in theology and has done additional post-graduate work in education, psychology, and counseling. He has been assistant professor of theology, director of a campus ministry center, National Consultant in Religion for an education division of CBS, and Executive for Program and rector in parish ministry. He has worked with Cursillo, Walk to Emmaus, and Kairos, as well as with various denominational judicatories in retreat and spiritual formation work.

An Episcopal priest, Ron leads retreats, conferences, and training events across the country in spirituality and pastoral care. He has been doing spiritual direction since 1965. Ron is active in ministry with the sick and the dying and involved in working for peace and justice. With his wife, Eleanor, he directs The Hermitage, a place for people to enter into solitude and prayer under their direction.

Ron and Eleanor live in Trussville, Alabama, and have two grown children, Paul and Anne.

Mary and Herb Montgomery are full-time writers who have created numerous books and educational projects to help both children and adults grow in faith. The Montgomerys live in Minneapolis.